Piecemeal

Ahana Banerji

Published by Nine Pens Press
2024
www.ninepens.co.uk

All rights reserved: no part of this book may be reproduced without the publisher's permission.
The right of the author to be identified as the author of this work has been asserted by them in accordance with the Copyright, Designs and Patents act 1988

ISBN: 978-1-917150-01-9

022

Contents

9 Mothering Sunday
10 Leaving tongues
11 Early days
12 Fishers
13 Notes on baptism
14 Devotional Poem
15 Heatwave
16 Afterwards
17 Three Imitations at the Ashmolean
18 A Dog Called Tuesday (i)
19 (ii)
20 Robbie's Dream
21 Elegy for Joan Didion
22 A Bedtime Story
25 Piecemeal
27 Villanelle from your small talk
28 Meditations from an Unfamiliar Floor
29 A Rib-Faced Doe in Clare College
30 Apology

for Ma

– All you ever do is rain!

– I'm sorry.

- *Hour of the Star,* Clarice Lispector

Mothering Sunday

Strong like the sun, or was it *like a son,*
you forget, denying the sting
at your throat. The sill homes butter-thin roses.
You refuse to name yourself
until you start mistaking my fingertips
for pomegranate pips. Only a daughter
will spend herself skimming
milk off your breath, spooling
your tempers in her body, revering
your reserve, almost losing it,
like the boundary of a freckle on our wrist.
I'm sorry for stealing your poetry.
You taught me so much, but little else.

Leaving tongues

You wrap my fingers in the leaves, wintergreen,
twisting psalms between loose teeth.

Bound, I swear to something sharp
as my father's nose, your mother's mouth.

You harvest my handship
before the bruising of the midrib,

as the kingfisher breaks
his bill on a bone-eared stone.

Minnows scarper upstream, no longer monarchs.
Beneath our casuarina tree, you are

deadheading asphodels. We watch
white tongues curdle by our feet.

Early days

Last week, I saw my first pumpkin patch.
The earth was scabby with them,
wounded and puckered and ready to hollow.

Some nights, you turn gourd
-heavy against me, too. My forehead
not quite flush against your chest

is also some mutable distance. Each morning,
I awake to more pencil under stanzas
where I've glassed your voice.

The seasons do not cry fast enough for us.
You are better off dreaming of afternoons
tender and amber as scrambled egg, just overdone.

Fishers
> *after García Lorca*

Tonight, Federico is in a fish market.
We study men scabbing scales off salmon,
weighing a pound of cheek against a gavel.
He's pretending not to notice me.

He's been trying to fry angelfish in the moon
for the past half an hour. I've just found the liver
to tell him this is as possible as bludgeoning freckles
to a son or restoring a voice to sea salt.

The moon, smooth as a sleeping back,
understands the pressure of unseen things
and curves duly. Once, it blared so bright
I thought it was electric.

This secret lives in me like a streetlight:
passed under, spinal, a constant in darkness.
Federico winks at me, angelfish still raw and oily.
Tells me to find my stomach.

Notes on baptism

Drying on the radiator, his jeans
drenched in a familiar heavy. I tell
a friend the grief will end but I am
not so sure. It overpurples. The water
smiles before it swallows. I do not
believe he slipped, I heard him say.
But that's grief, was the reply. That's
untrusting, said the water.

Devotional Poem

And I am telling you   about temple
I want   to paint   marigolds
with my tongue   instead
googling   *amrita sher-gil*
we stare at   self-portraits   for an hour

I am still   telling you   about temple
once   I prayed   for you   because
it   was   a butchery
that obituary   was so long ago   now

I am telling   you   about temple
how   Kali loaned me   this body   I could be
an ant   between your fingers   and still burn
but   destruction   is not   to be feared
this is   the only baptism   I understand

Heatwave

This heat has made an animal of me!
Bluebottles marble my knuckles, studs of opal.

I tried to tell you stories but instead
we lounged like a pride, horribly mammal.

Pen dribbles like pork fat across the page.
All the better to anoint you with, my dear.

Dimly, I remember the winter you loved me best,
wiped my running nose. Now,

I am brushing gnats off
my poems all by myself.

*This heat is a blanket
of death,* you say, soft as pampas.

I ask if that's a promise.
There is no wind to carry your voice.

Afterwards

I lie in bed, waiting for you –
pressing oil
under my right wrist,
over orphaned petechiae,
into the reddish band below my breasts –
I am trying to define these lines
between buying violets for a date
and eyeing tulips on the bedside –

[…]

Remember those kids who called us fags?
Fear fell from them like milk teeth!
Those little petrol-stink apostles make me
wonder if confessing me to you
would steward the sea, dam the moat,
unpool the bruise between us –
But you are not God. I am still not well.
And I lie in bed, waiting for you –

Three Imitations at the Ashmolean

'Nude on a Sofa', Matisse
I'm sorry he lost your name but kept your hat. He unbuttons that blister on your ankle, tempers that tempera bruise with his *reduced palette*. When you stand, your menstrual blood satiates the negative space. You will learn to fix your hat without his mirror, someday.

'The Artist's Mother', Laurencin
You accept a small apology for the light. You have tried to alphabetise your jokes, but they are stitched like sinew in the shelf, warmed by morning. Before your daughter, an understanding. Some are built only to hold themselves.

'Interior with Nude Figure', Bonnard
I regret to inform you that this room won't hold you much longer. You try to see yourself, predict the blue knuckle of your hips, the indigo dimples of your thighs. He calls your hair ostrich-feather! And yes, some flightless wing enters you. He completes you without knowing the colour of your eyes.

A Dog Called Tuesday (i)

All canines biting in the mind, you say, wrestling it small.
It's difficult to trust your poetry
when you haven't brushed your teeth in three days.

The edge of your bed is like the corner of your mouth:
damp, tired, grey. You are still trying
to deny that animal and I feel too slight to prey.

It has swollen so impossibly, though
your ribs are gnawing through your t-shirt.
It is festering. Mushroom sinister, elbow soft.

I want to make you oil-clean,
but the heat of my thumb has become
another fact you can't stand.

Eyeing my silence, you tell me to leave,
your skin burning static beneath your sleeve.

(ii)

You stain, coffee on cotton,
caffeinating through conversation.

Now, your period is more
than an omen we shared.

Six years I've watched you
deny yourself, over and over:

who fed you that diet
of pressing violets, pushing violence,

pulling lightning like tablets under
the tongue? I can't recognise the eyes

stuck to the pockmarked calendar.
Mug on your Gideon's, you are swearing

to bleed over and over again.

Robbie's Dream

I called Robbie today. We mused the future, for the first time. He says that one day, he'll teach Physics. Live in Skye. Marry Teo in a church that loves so despite-heavy. I'll wear silk shirts & visit them for amber-lit dinners – eat carrots and grapes with hot gravy, yoghurt with honey. They'll have three dogs – Ottolenghi, Ripley, Pavarotti – & we'll go stargazing, together. We'll talk about *Americanah*, about how lucky we are to still be in touch, to have survived our grey days, those white mouths

Elegy for Joan Didion

Joan Didion!
Am I with you in Ernie's,
      where you dyed your roots blue?
Am I with you in Ernie's,
      writing a novel in your alphabet soup?
Am I with you in Ernie's,
      mistaking ketchup for blood on the gums?
Am I with you in Ernie's,
      with those other unexfoliated serpents?

Oh, Joan. While you are ash-safe, I am oil-safe,
so now we're prized in this great, burgundy lapse of mine,
minding the screech of the tar-veined highway.
In my dreams, you talk through Malibu sunshine
with warm linen in your mouth,
clean shroud. So embarrassingly soft.

A Bedtime Story

Mother and daughter share a bed,
sleepless in the unfamiliar night-time heat.

Daughter leans her cheek against the cool,
iron-barred window, feeling the thick breeze
and watching trucks scrape dust on the tracks.

Mother turns, a warm shift in the shadows
and a pale scent of lemon and salt,
and tugs daughter down, back onto the bed-sweat.

Daughter begs mother to tell her a story,
her voice thin against the shroud of air.

Mother sighs, and presses her lips
to daughter's ear, and whispers,

— Do you know why the banyan tree cries?

Mother traces daughter's temple with her fingertip.

— The banyan bears fruit – not sweet like mango, or curative like amla, but bitter and bloodshot like an eye, bulging. It rots always because it can only be stomached in the worst of all famines.

Mother wraps her arm around daughter like a root.

— I was around your age when it happened. I was walking home from school, kicking stones so hard they slit the leather of my shoe, when I passed the banyan tree. A woman was perched in its ropes, so old she wrinkled like a shawl and she waved to me - *Beta*, she called, *I climbed the banyan to pluck its harvest, but my sandals slipped as I clambered. Will you pick them up for me? Put them on my feet before you go?* The sandals were brown and tough, caked in earth and car oil, but I did as I was told. She swung her legs over the branch with her hands the same way a fishmonger might slam his catch onto the ice. That is when the banyan started to cry, as she presented me with two stumps, raw and blunt as mutton, and I dropped the sandals and ran as fast and far away as I could.

Daughter nuzzles into mother's breast,
her small breaths drubbing like a heartbeat.

— Do you understand, now, why the banyan tree cries? It has so many hungry souls trapped in its belly, it has forgotten how to feed itself. The cowardly, the liars, the witches, and the whores – they all have nowhere and no one who wants them, so, into the belly of the banyan they go where their tears turn cold and plump the fruit of the banyan tree.

Daughter, too, spends the night steeping salt in her teeth, and mother settles into sleep, heavy with new grief.

Piecemeal

Two dozen frozen prawns float grey & knuckled
like a storm in a glass bowl, arthritic thunderclouds.

Across my palm the scissors lie flat,
lines fattening under its weight.

My mother startles mustard seed for tadka.
She taught me how to trust a blade to

never cut you even when
it's pressed all up against you.

Over the rumbling cooker
we talk like TV so loud & lyric:

*Your father he says he is tired. Well guess what
daddy I am also, I am also done.*

Our men kitchen themselves in this conversation.
Anointing your name is solace in her company.

Mid-mutilation I confess the peripherals of you:
how we ate bunsik near the Embankment, our love of Lorca.

My mother is careful not to touch me.
Her excuse is allergy & the instinct to starve herself

if it means feeding others. She reminds me hunger
is a learned thing. Meeting heat the prawns pinken.

Turning the tap, I baptise threads
of black intestine out of my fingernails.

Villanelle from your small talk

Day-old daylilies. Lobster in Maine.
Finding comfort in a conversation's guillotines,
learning to confess again.

Your same-
self demeanour seems
like day-old daylilies. Lobster in Maine.

Seeking Jesus in a red wine stain,
you forget my carpet cannot make you clean.
You're still learning to confess again.

Wisteria strains
into silkscreen.
Day-old daylilies. Lobster in Maine.

What uncanny membrane
did you collapse into sunbeam?
Learning to confess again,

the meadow-heart is reduced to grain
until the sapling, too, is seen.
Day-old daylilies. Lobster in Maine.
As if learning to confess again.

Meditations from an Unfamiliar Floor

These walls don't sink.

Something has been ripped from this doorframe
and it was probably *Pulp Fiction*.

I spider myself
into one too many corners.

I have known more than my own
but I do not own it well. These walls

upset themselves like glasses
of water in the night. I become into window-

box. The small carnation of my breast
shudders white and fingernail.

I could turn against even November for light.
I'm as safe looking in as out,

ignoring myself into carpet. These walls
will know me over and over

before the gentle keeping of these little hours.

A Rib-Faced Doe in Clare College

So small between the milkweed,
those little fists of feverfew,
our ribs deciduous.

We watched her stumble into green.
Your ear thistles with hearing lost things.
My pockets parsley with an illegible psalter.

Tender is the oak in October. We know.
But we do not approve. The overgrowth can hold her only.
You would have missed her, without me.

Apology

And there will always be new cold
on the windowsill, new gentle
splintered fingernail, the little frost.
So razor fresh. So crocus fresh.

I am sorry for the iris heat of yesterday
and nothing more. I mistake
a riverbed knuckled with fish
for something simple. I, too, will be

good. Good
as the jugular's perfect hyacinth.
Small budding. Smalling disappointments.
I know. And I am not resigned.

Notes

Previous versions of some of these poems have appeared with The Poetry Society's Young Poets Network, *The White Review*, *Anthropocene*, *the Tower Poetry Prize 2020*, *Zindabad*, and *Bad Lilies*.

'Three Imitations at the Ashmolean Museum' refers to three portraits by Henri Matisse, Marie Laurencin, and Pierre Bonnard on display in the Ashmolean Museum in Oxford as of August 2022.

The line 'collapse into sunbeam' in 'Villanelle from your small talk' is altered from the Arlo Parks album 'Collapsed in Sunbeams', which in turn is taken from an image in Zadie Smith's novel 'On Beauty'.

'Elegy for Joan Didion' is written after the third part of Allen Ginsberg's 'Howl'. The line 'So embarrassingly soft' is from Nina Simone's performance of 'Feelings' Live at Montreux in 1976.

The final stanza of 'A Rib-Faced Doe in Clare College' is shaped by Edna St. Vincent Millay's poem 'Dirge Without Music'. 'Apology' also takes its final line from this poem.

Acknowledgments

Many of these poems would not exist without my best friend/editor/companion Leo Kang. Thank you.

And of course, to my family for their unending support - especially my Ma, Erika, who taught me how to write. Thank you for giving me Dickinson and Plath to read ~~when I was too young~~ at a formative age.

www.ingramcontent.com/pod-product-compliance
Lightning Source LLC
Chambersburg PA
CBHW030136100526
44591CB00009B/682